discovermore
Earth Science

Weather and Climate

Theia Lake

Britannica Educational Publishing

IN ASSOCIATION WITH

THE ROSEN PUBLISHING GROUP

Published in 2026 by Britannica Educational Publishing (a trademark of Encyclopædia Britannica, Inc.) in association with The Rosen Publishing Group, Inc.
2544 Clinton Street, Buffalo, NY 14224

Distributed exclusively by Rosen Publishing.
To see additional Britannica Educational Publishing titles, go to rosenpublishing.com.

Editor: Danielle Haynes
Book Design: Michael Flynn

Photo Credits: Cover Shutterstock.com; (series background) Dai Yim/Shutterstock.com; p. 4 TORWAISTUDIO/Shutterstock.com; p. 5 PeopleImages.com - Yuri A/Shutterstock.com; p. 6 Lukasz Pawel Szczepanski/Shutterstock.com; p. 7 Yevhen Prozhyrko/Shutterstock.com; p. 8 Digi.Pixel/Shutterstock.com; p. 9 MantasVD/Shutterstock.com; p. 10 Shestak Vera/Shutterstock.com; p. 11 AZ Septian/Shutterstock.com; p. 12 HappyBall3692/Shutterstock.com; p. 13 Shovon SIS/Shutterstock.com; p. 14 idea _Photo/Shutterstock.com; p. 15 New Africa/Shutterstock.com; p. 16 Triff/Shutterstock.com; p. 17 witorn/Shutterstock.com; p. 19 (top) irin-k/Shutterstock.com; p. 19 (bottom) rzoze19/Shutterstock.com; p. 21 (top) semper-scifi/Shutterstock.com; p. 21 (bottom) FiledIMAGE/Shutterstock.com; p. 22 Ursula Page/Shutterstock.com; p. 23 Mirko Graul/Shutterstock.com; p. 25 Mihai_Andritoiu/Shutterstock.com; p. 26 Nancy Pauwels/Shutterstock.com; p. 27 wsf-s/Shutterstock.com; p. 28 NadyGinzburg/Shutterstock.com; p. 29 Sergey Novikov/Shutterstock.com.

Cataloging-in-Publication Data

Names: Lake, Theia.
Title: Weather and climate / Theia Lake.
Description: New York : Britannica Educational Publishing, in association with Rosen Educational Services, 2026. | Series: Discover more: earth science | Includes glossary and index.
Identifiers: ISBN 9781641904346 (library bound) | ISBN 9781641904339 (pbk) | ISBN 9781641904353 (ebook)
Subjects: LCSH: Weather--Juvenile literature. | Climatology--Juvenile literature.
Classification: LCC QC981.3 L35 2026 | DDC 551.6--dc23

Manufactured in the United States of America

CPSIA Compliance Information: Batch #CSBRIT26. For further information contact Rosen Publishing at 1-800-237-9932.

Contents

The Weather and You

When you wake up in the morning, how do you know what kind of clothes to put on for the day? Do you need a jacket? An umbrella? First, you must check the weather. Weather is the state of the atmosphere at any given time and place. It has a huge effect on our lives. Heavy rain can spoil your plans for a day out. Cold weather can kill a farmer's plants. A sunny day can make people feel more cheerful.

A rainy day calls for raincoats and umbrellas.

Sunny days call for shorts and T-shirts.

There are many different types of weather. The weather can be hot, cold, or somewhere in between. It can also be dry, humid or wet, sunny, partly cloudy, or gray. Weather affects our lives in many ways, but what causes different types of weather? Let's take a look at the science of weather!

Consider This

As you read this book, think about how different types of weather are connected. For example, how are sun and wind connected?

The Sun's Heat

The sun, which is a star, is one of the single biggest influences on the Earth's weather. A star is a giant ball of burning gas. The sun is the nearest star to Earth. Like other stars, the sun gives off huge amounts of heat and light energy. The sun is about 93 million miles (150 million km) from Earth but still provides our planet with its heat and light!

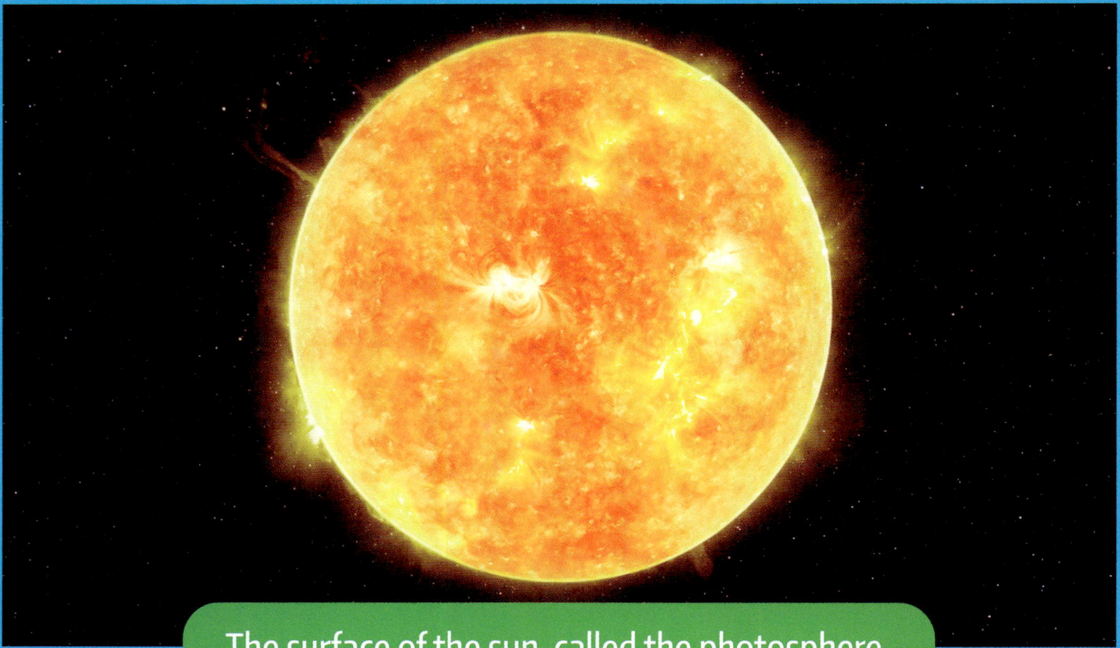

The surface of the sun, called the photosphere, is 10,000°Fahrenheit (5,500°Celsius).

The sun's rays can damage and burn our skin with too much exposure. Sunblock can help protect us from the harmful effects.

The sun makes it warm enough for living things to survive on Earth. Plants use sunlight to make food and grow. People need plants to eat and to feed the animals that we eat. Without the sun, there would be no plants, animals, or humans.

Consider This

The light and heat from the sun are very strong. Why do you think people should wear sunblock on hot, sunny days?

The Atmosphere Around Us

The Earth's atmosphere is a layer of gases that surrounds the planet and protects it from the sun's most harmful rays. The atmosphere helps keep the world warm. When heat energy from the sun warms Earth's surface, the warm land heats the air above it. Warm air rises, so some heat escapes into space. The atmosphere also reflects heat back toward Earth, which helps to keep us warm.

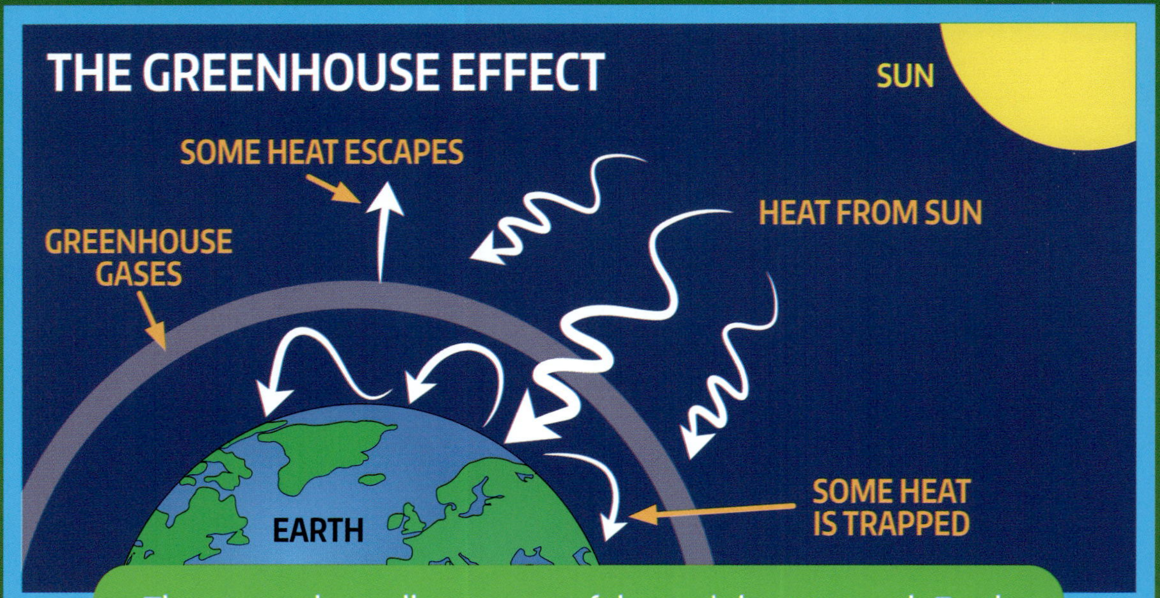

The atmosphere allows some of the sun's heat to reach Earth but keeps more harmful rays and radiation out of the planet.

Here, a storm brews in the Earth's atmosphere.

All of Earth's weather happens in the lowest part of the atmosphere, closest to Earth. This layer of air can be wet, dry, hot, cold, moving, or still. The changes in this layer of the atmosphere give us our many different types of weather.

The weight of the air above a given area is called atmospheric pressure. Changes in pressure help people to predict approaching storms. Storms are major disturbances within the atmosphere that usually involve rain or some other kind of precipitation, wind, thunder, and lightning.

Consider This

When people burn fuels, they put more gases into the atmosphere. What effect do you think this might have on the amount of heat the atmosphere traps on Earth?

Cloudy Skies

Clouds are tiny water droplets or ice crystals in the Earth's atmosphere. Clouds form when the sun warms Earth's surface. Heat from the ground then warms the air just above it. When warm air rises and moves high up in the sky, it cools down again. This turns **water vapor** in the air into tiny drops of water. These drops of water collect together and form clouds.

Many clouds start to form above oceans, where most water evaporates. Wind blows the vapor over land, where we see clouds gathering.

WORD WISE

WATER VAPOR IS THE GAS THAT FORMS WHEN WATER IS HEATED.

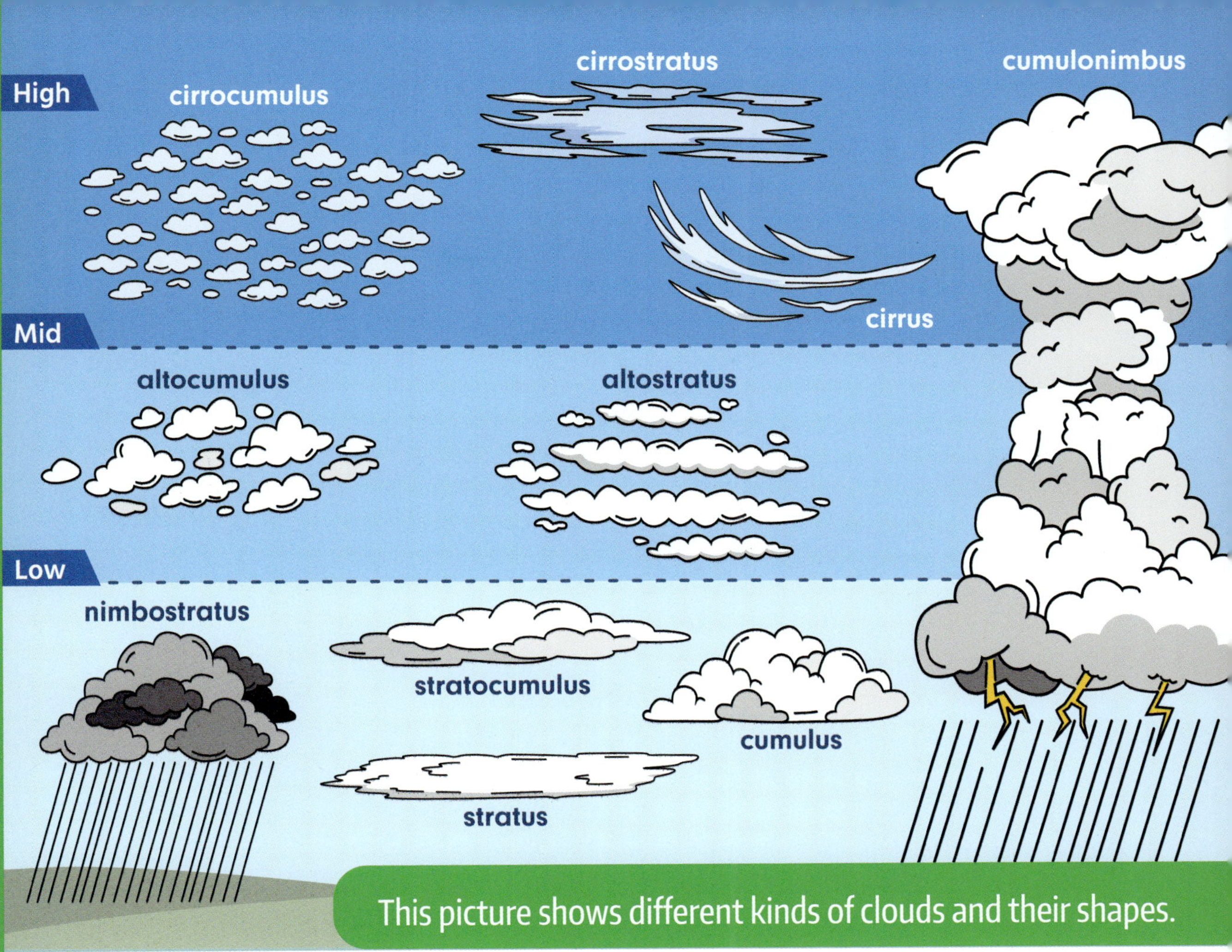

This picture shows different kinds of clouds and their shapes.

The three main types of clouds are cirrus, cumulus, and stratus. Cirrus clouds are high, thin clouds made up of ice crystals. Cumulus clouds are puffy clouds that are often piled up like mountains. Stratus clouds are flat layers of clouds. Nimbus is the Latin word for rain. A cumulonimbus cloud is a type of raincloud. They can differ greatly in size and appearance.

Rain and Rainbows

Sometimes clouds bring rain and other kinds of precipitation. Rain is a part of Earth's endless water cycle. At the beginning of the cycle, sunlight heats up water on Earth's surface. The heat causes the water to evaporate, or turn into water vapor. This water vapor rises into the air. As the water vapor cools, it turns back into water in the form of droplets.

Rain is important for bringing water to plants, animals, and humans.

Rainbows form when light from the sun comes into contact with tiny drops of water in the air. Sunlight looks clear, but it is made up of different colors. When sunlight passes through the droplets, the water bends the light and splits it into different colors. You'll also see rainbows when light passes through certain kinds of windows and prisms.

Consider This

Why do you usually see rainbows after it rains?

Frozen Precipitation

In addition to rain, there are many kinds of frozen precipitation. Snow forms when the **temperature** of the sky is so cold that the water vapor in a cloud freezes. It turns from liquid water into tiny pieces of solid ice. The pieces of ice stick together and form snowflakes. When they become big and heavy, they fall from the sky.

If the temperature on the ground is below freezing, the snow won't melt when it lands.

Hailstones can be as large as tennis balls or even bigger!

Hail forms in giant cumulonimbus clouds. Fast winds in these clouds blow raindrops up into the top layers of the clouds. There, the air is so cold that it turns the raindrops into small balls of ice, called hailstones. They swirl around in the cloud, bump into each other, and join together. When they become too heavy to float, they fall to the ground. Some hailstones are small and may look like snow. Others are large and can cause lots of damage.

WORD WISE

TEMPERATURE IS HOW HOT OR COLD SOMETHING IS.

Lightning and Thunder

Along with precipitation, cumulonimbus clouds produce thunder and lightning. These huge, dark clouds can reach from the ground to high in the sky. Winds blow tiny pieces of ice around in the clouds. When the pieces of ice rub against each other, they cause **static electricity**. If the electricity in the clouds builds up, it can cause a flash of lightning.

Lightning is a path of electricity between the sky and the ground.

If struck, lightning rods conduct the electricity to the ground through a wire.

Lightning is very, very hot. As it travels through the air, it makes the air around it hot, too. This makes the air expand suddenly, which causes the loud bang that we call thunder.

If lightning hits a building, it can cause a fire. Today, many buildings have lightning rods. They carry the electricity from a lightning strike safely into the ground. This stops the lightning from setting the building on fire. Lightning rods have a wire that connects them to the ground, where the energy from the lightning is safely dispersed.

WORD WISE

STATIC ELECTRICITY IS A TYPE OF ELECTRICITY USUALLY CAUSED BY THINGS RUBBING TOGETHER.

Morning Frost and Dew

Sometimes when you wake up in the morning, the ground looks a little different than when you went to bed. Frost and dew form in the morning after a night during which the air has been cold and the sky clear. On nights such as this, the land gets colder than the air above it. Frost forms when water vapor near the ground meets very cold surfaces. The water vapor turns into tiny pieces of ice.

Dew forms on nights when the air near the ground is full of water vapor. When the temperature drops at night, water vapor in the air becomes cold and turns into drops of water. These drops of water are near to the ground, so they often gather on surfaces such as grass. The temperature at which dew forms is called the dew point, which can vary greatly from day to day and place to place.

Frost usually doesn't last long and often melts once the sun comes out.

compare and contrast

How are frost and dew similar? How are they different?

Dew collects on trees, grass, and even spiderwebs!

Fog and Mist

Weather conditions can sometimes make the world look a little creepy. Mist and fog occur when the air is humid, or full of moisture, making tiny drops of water float in the air near Earth's surface. When water vapor just above the ground or over the sea meets a layer of cold air, the water vapor turns into tiny droplets of water. The droplets stay so small that they are light enough to float in the air. When fog is so thin that we can see through it, it is called mist.

Fog is thicker than mist, and it can be dangerous. Fog can make it difficult for drivers to see where they are going at night, when it is also dark. Both fog and mist are more likely to occur in warm weather, since warm air can hold more moisture than cold air can. Fog usually clears up in direct sunlight.

Mist is thin enough that you can usually see through it.

compareandcontrast

How are fog and mist similar to rain? How are they different?

Fog is denser than mist and can be very dangerous to drive in.

The Power of Wind

Wind is moving air that happens when there are changes in air pressure. Air moves because heat from the sun creates different temperatures, which cause that change in pressure. Sunlight warms the ground and then the air above the ground becomes warmer. When warm air rises, cool air moves in to fill the space the warm air has left behind. As the warm air rises, it gets cooler and sinks again. This moving air is wind. Winds may be gentle or powerful.

Wind can be so strong it can knock down trees or lift roofs from houses during a storm.

The power of wind can also be captured by windmills to be turned into electricity.

Areas of land, such as streets and fields, heat up faster in the sun than water does. That is why it is usually cooler at the coast than it is inland. When warm air above land rises, cooler air from the sea blows in to fill the space that the warm air leaves behind. This makes a cool sea breeze. Wind is invisible, but we can feel its effects and see the things it moves.

Consider This

How do you think wind causes waves on the ocean?

Changing Seasons

Each year is broken down into seasons in which the weather changes. Seasons change because Earth is tilted as it moves around the sun every year. This means that different parts of the planet get different amounts of sunlight during the year. For example, between March and August, the Northern Hemisphere is tilted toward the sun, so this is when the lands there have their warm spring and summer seasons.

The changing seasons bring changes to plants and animal life. In summer, there are more hours of sunlight, so this is when plants grow the most. In winter, there are fewer hours of sunlight, so some plants die. They grow again in spring. During the fall, or autumn, temperatures grow cooler and the leaves on trees change colors.

In the winter (top left), snow covers the ground in many places. In spring (bottom left), many plants bloom such as this cherry tree. In summer (top right), things get much warmer, while in fall (bottom right), the leaves turn colors in preparation for colder months.

compare and contrast

How do trees and plants look in spring and summer?
How do they look in fall and winter?

Earth's Climates

Climate is different than weather in that it's the usual type of weather in a specific area. Weather, on the other hand, refers to the conditions at a specific time. A country's climate tells you how hot, cold, wet, or snowy it is likely to be there at different times of the year. For example, a region may have cold winters and hot, dry summers. In some places, the climate stays the same all year. For example, deserts are almost always dry, and Antarctica is always cold.

The climate at the Earth's poles, such as in Antarctica, shown here, is cold and has very few, if any, plants.

Most tropical vacation spots, such as Addu Atoll in the Maldives, are located on or near the equator where the climate is hot.

The usual temperatures of a place depend on the place's position on Earth. For example, the area around the **equator** is always hot. Our planet is shaped like a ball, but the sun's light and heat energy travel to Earth in a straight line. This means the energy strikes the equator directly, making it the hottest place on Earth. The North and South Poles, however, get very little of that direct sunlight so they're cold and snowy.

WORD WISE

THE EQUATOR IS AN IMAGINARY LINE AROUND THE MIDDLE OF EARTH.

Climate Change

You probably hear a lot about climate change in the news and at school. World climates change over thousands or millions of years. Today, however, our climate is changing very quickly. When people burn fuels such as coal, oil, and natural gas in engines and power stations, a gas called carbon dioxide is released. The gas escapes into the air and then into the atmosphere. There, it traps more heat on Earth. This is making Earth hotter and hotter.

Gas-powered vehicles release carbon emissions into the air, which fuels climate change and can make people sick.

Instead of getting a ride to school in a car, think about riding your bike or walking to avoid contributing to gas emissions.

Higher temperatures on Earth cause more extreme weather. There are more forest fires. Droughts cause plants to die because they do not have enough water. Stronger storms cause floods and blow down trees, damaging buildings. People are now trying to slow climate change, for example, by making electricity using the power of wind or sun instead of burning fuels. This type of fuel is called renewable because it's unlikely we'll ever run out of wind or sunlight to make more energy.

Consider This

What can you do to slow down climate change?

Glossary

carbon dioxide A colorless, odorless gas found in the atmosphere.
dense The state of being compact or thick.
disperse To cause to break up or spread widely.
disturbance The interruption of peace and quiet, in this case the weather.
droplet A very small drop of water.
drought A long period of dry weather.
emissions The greenhouse gases released into the air by vehicles and other machinery.
exposure The act of being unprotected.
humid Damp or moist.
lightning A giant spark of electricity between a cloud and the ground.
precipitation The liquid and solid water particles that fall from clouds and reach the ground.
predict To guess what will happen in the future based on facts or knowledge.
prism A transparent object, often a crystal, that disperses light.
radiation Waves of energy.
sunblock A type of lotion that protects the skin from the sun's harmful rays.

For More Information

Books

Earley, Christina. *Climate*. Coral Springs, FL: Seahorse Publishing, 2024.

Finan, Catherine C. *Weather*. Minneapolis, MN: Bearport Publishing Company, 2021.

Woodward, John. *Climate Change*. New York, NY: DK Publishing, 2021.

Websites

NASA: Climate Kids
www.climatekids.nasa.gov/menu/weather-and-climate
Read more about the different kinds of weather and climate patterns on this NASA website.

National Geographic Kids: What Is Climate Change?
www.natgeokids.com/uk/discover/geography/general-geography/what-is-climate-change
Learn more about how to stop climate change.

Index